T0000316

A DOG RUNS

THROUGH IT

A DOG RUNS THROUGH IT

Poems

Linda Pastan

W. W. NORTON & COMPANY

Independent Publishers Since 1923

New York | London

Copyright © 2018 by Linda Pastan
Illustrations copyright © 2018 by W. W. Norton & Company, Inc.

All rights reserved
Printed in the United States of America
First Edition

For information about permission to reproduce selections
from this book, write to Permissions, W. W. Norton & Company, Inc.,
500 Fifth Avenue, New York, NY 10110

For information about special discounts for bulk purchases,
please contact W. W. Norton Special Sales at
specialsales@wwnorton.com or 800-233-4830

Manufacturing by Versa Press
Illustrations by Elsa Senner
Book design by Chris Welch Design
Production manager: Julia Druskin

Library of Congress Cataloging-in-Publication Data

Names: Pastan, Linda, date- author.
Title: A dog runs through it : poems / Linda Pastan.
Description: First edition. | New York : W. W. Norton & Company, [2018]
Identifiers: LCCN 2018002468 | ISBN 9780393651300 (hardcover)
Classification: LCC PS3566.A775 A6 2018 | DDC 811/.54—dc23
LC record available at https://lccn.loc.gov/2018002468

W. W. Norton & Company, Inc., 500 Fifth Avenue, New York, N.Y. 10110
www.wwnorton.com

W. W. Norton & Company Ltd., 15 Carlisle Street, London W1D 3BS

1 2 3 4 5 6 7 8 9 0

for Toby

CONTENTS

PREFACE

My first dog was named Rowdy. I was ten, an only child, and my parents thought a dog would be good company. But I had books for company. I wanted to sit under the shadow of the piano and simply read. Instead I had to walk the dog before I left for school and walk him again when I came home. The Grand Concourse, in the Bronx where we lived, had few trees. Rowdy would pee against apartment houses, against the tires of cars, and when people looked on disapprovingly I would pretend it was not me at the other end of the leash. Why didn't I love Rowdy more? He was a black and white wire-haired terrier with a square face, handsome and well behaved, and I had few other things in my life to love. I have paid dearly for that deficiency by loving the dogs who followed him all too passionately, all too well.

There was the Welsh terrier Rusty, in my teens, also square faced but black and orange. I tried to teach him tricks; I even took him to an obedience class. But my father undid all my careful training by roughhousing with him and repeating the commands I had taught him as if they were jokes. I suffered and suffered more when I had to leave home for college, knowing that my dog would be both neglected and spoiled. When I learned, in my sophomore year, that the boy I was dating also had a dog named Rusty, I married him.

Una was the first dog of our married life, a Bedlington terrier who looked like a lamb. On Halloween we put a sign around the dog's neck: "Wolf in Sheep's Clothing." I named Una for a character in *The Fairie Queen*, though everyone thought I had named her for Charlie Chaplin's wife Oona. But I had young children then, and I fear that though loved, Una was somewhat neglected in the chaos of family life.

Mowgli came next, the dog of my life. I say that in the spirit of a woman saying of a certain man: he was the love of my life. Mowgli was a Rhodesian ridgeback, bred to hunt lions in Africa. He was a large, rust-colored hound with a swordlike ridge of hair growing down his back. Though fierce looking, he was gentle and loving, and he followed me around the house from task to task—from laundry to study to kitchen. Once, when he disappeared for three days, I spent hours searching the woods near our house, shouting his name and weeping copiously. My husband finally found him in a deep hole some builder had dug to test the soil for a septic tank. He borrowed a ladder and carried Mowgli up in his arms. A few years later, though, when we were out of town, Mowgli died of stomach torsion while in a boarding kennel. I have never put a dog in a kennel again.

Caleb was another ridgeback, one with what John Irving called terminal flatulence, modeling a dog after him in *The Hotel New Hampshire*. My daughter Rachel was eleven when we got Caleb, but he was too big to sit on her lap. It was a lap dog she really wanted, so we added a black miniature poodle, Tanya, to our family. He lived with us for twenty-one years, longer than any of our children did.

Annie was our penultimate dog, a Norwich terrier. She looked a little like a large Toto—a cairn terrier.

I had seen one of her brothers at a friend's house, perfectly trained, sitting and lying down and rolling over on command. Perhaps I thought Norwich terriers were born that way. Annie certainly wasn't, but she was an easy and lovable dog, though she would drink water only if someone was petting her. People told me that she would drink if she became thirsty enough, but that was like telling me to let my baby cry himself to sleep, something I had never done.

And now we have Toby, our rescue dog, a gray mini-poodle mix. He is a bit longer than the usual mini-poodle, so perhaps there is some dachshund in his DNA. Our whole family seems to be rescuing dogs recently, a fine trend, and Toby is a delight. But we had been told he was six years old, and when later our vet told us he must be at least ten, it was too late to consider returning him. He might not live for many years, but then neither might we, and in any case, we were hooked.

What is it about dogs anyway, and dog people? We know who we are. We stop strangers on the street who just happen to be walking a dog, and we talk to them. We hang out in dog parks. We cross a street to greet an unknown dog on the other side. And when a dog appears early in a movie, we worry that something will happen to it by the end. In fact, someone has actually made an app where you can put in the name of a movie and it will tell you if the dog is going to die!

Some dog people have a kind of natural authority with dogs; dogs just know to obey them. I am not one of those people. I am more like the substitute teacher who walks into a classroom and every student relaxes and starts to text. My dogs jump on me, bark at me, pull on the leash when we walk. So why am I hooked?

President Truman was supposedly told that if you want to have a friend in Washington, you should get a dog. I live in Washington too, or nearby anyway, but I have lots of friends, so that's not it. Nor is it simply the wish to have company or to be unconditionally loved. It's something much more instinctive, even primal. Perhaps when our ancestors were domesticating dogs by long-ago campfires, a process that took years, we were learning to need them as they would learn to need us.

And so to this book. I knew I had written a

number of poems about dogs over the years, but I was surprised when looking through my work to see how many dogs had sneaked onto a page about something else entirely, making the briefest of appearances. It reminded me of Toby, sneaking onto the forbidden couch when nobody was watching. This book is dedicated to him.

A DOG RUNS

THROUGH IT

The Great Dog of Night

John Wilde, oil on panel

The great dog of night
growls at the windows,
barks at the door.

Soon I must straddle
its sleek back and fly
over the fields

and rooftops
of sleep, above us
a vague moon

loose in the sky,
far ahead of us
morning.

The New Dog

Into the gravity of my life,
the serious ceremonies
of polish and paper and pen, has come

this manic animal
whose innocent disruptions
make nonsense
of my old simplicities

as if I needed him
to prove again that after
all the careful planning
anything can happen.

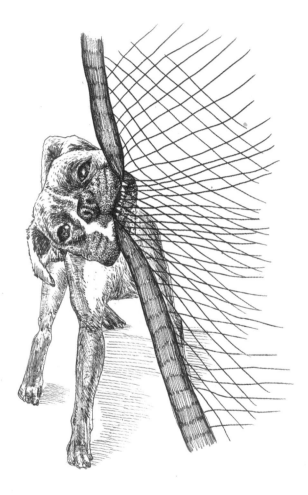

In the Garden

I tell my dog to sit
and he sits
and I give him
a biscuit.
I tell him to come
and he comes
and sits,
and I give him
a biscuit
again.
I tell my dog Lie Down!
and he sits,
looking up
at me with trust
and adoration.
I pause.
I give him
a biscuit.
This is the beginning
of love and
disobedience.
I was never meant
to be a god.

Departures

My dog barks under an empty tree
long after the squirrel has gone.
He barks and barks, and the squirrel
leaps ten trees away, leaving
the leaf tops trembling like trampolines
after an acrobat is through.
And he stands gazing up at her
who long ago stopped loving him
while that foolish dog still barks.

Heartbeat

The book says:
give the pup
a ticking clock to sleep with,
he'll think
that it's his mother.

When she left
he tried
a different life,
a different lover,
a ticking
clock.

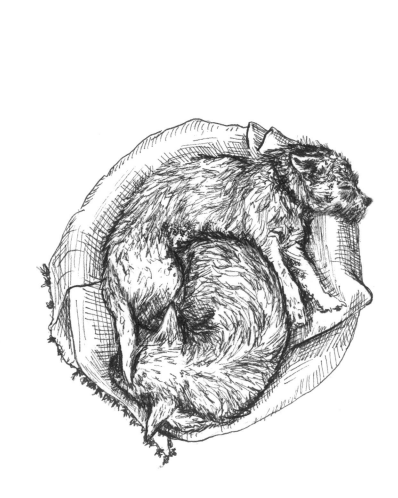

Domestic Animals

The animals in this house
have dream claws and teeth
and shadow the rooms
at night, their furled tails dangerous.
In the morning, all sweet slobber,
the dog may yawn, the cat
make cat sounds deep
in its furred throat.
And who would guess
how they wait for dark
when into the green
jungle of our sleep
they insinuate
themselves, releasing
their terrible hunger.

In the Walled Garden

In the walled garden
where my illusions grow,
the lilac, watered, blooms all winter,
and innocence grows like moss
on the north side of every tree.
No ax or mower resides here—
green multiplies unimpeded—
and every morning all the dogs
of my long life jump up
to lick my face.
My father rests behind a hedge,
bard of my storied childhood,
and in the fading half life of ambition,
wanting and having merge.
Here flowers and flesh don't wither.
Here you will never leave me.
Here poetry will save the world.

Rivermist: for Roland Flint

When the kennel where my ridgeback died
some thirty years ago, wrote
to ask for my business again,
offering us one free night's board
for every three nights paid, I looked
at that name on the envelope: Rivermist,
imagining they were writing to say
that Mowgli was somehow alive,
the swordlike blade of fur still bristling
on his back; that he had waited
all these years for me to pick him up.
And though I've had four dogs since,
a small one at my feet right now, each
running too swiftly through his life and mine,
I could have wept, thinking of rivers and mists—
how in their wavering shadows
they had prefigured and concealed
the losses to come: mother and uncles, friends,
and Roland now, so newly dead, who
on the flyleaf of an early book once wrote,
in his careful, redemptive hand: with love

for Linda and Ira, and for Mowgli.

On Seeing *The Glass Menagerie*:
New York, 1946

How did he know about my glass animals,
the way I dusted each one lovingly—the elephant
with its transparent curve of trunk, the blue-eyed hen,
the poodle with its curled, spun-sugar topknot?

How did he know about the awkward boys
who came to the door,
sons of my mother's friends,
coerced into asking me out?

Ah, fragile zoo! Ah, adolescent callers!
I saw that play and knew that someone
understood me, knew that I could hide
in language the rest of my life.

I Am Learning to Abandon the World: for M

I am learning to abandon the world
before it can abandon me.
Already I have given up the moon
and snow, closing my shades
against the claims of white.
And the world has taken
my father, my friend.
I have given up melodic lines of hills,
moving to a flat, tuneless landscape.
And every night I give my body up
limb by limb, working upward
across bone, toward the heart.
But morning comes with small
reprieves of coffee and birdsong.
A tree outside the window
which was simply shadow moments ago
takes back its branches twig
by leafy twig.
And as I take my body back
the sun lays its warm muzzle on my lap
as if to make amends.

Patterns

The way the gulls' tracks in sand—
pattern of bisected triangles—are erased
by the breaking waves;

my mother pinning
the Vogue pattern onto the silky
blue fabric;

the long marching band of numbers: 4
is the square of 2, 16 the square
of 4, and so on;

sex and Samoa—
our adolescent take
on Patterns of Culture;

how history repeats itself:
war, and famine, and quiet
spells of peace;

our fragile days together: toast
and the morning paper, work
and wine and walking the dog

who marks
the usual hydrant, lamppost,
spindly tree.

What mortal patterns wait
in these aromatic tea leaves, in these
indelible lines mapping my palm?

McGuffey's First Eclectic Reader

The sun is up,
the sun is always up.
The silent "e"
keeps watch,
and 26 strong stones
can build a wall of syllables
for Nell and Ned
and Ann.

Rab was such a good dog,
Mother. We left him
under the big tree
by the brook
to take care of the dolls
and the basket.

But Rab has run away.
The basket's gone back to reeds
through which the night wind
blows; and mother was erased;
the dolls are painted harlots
in the Doll's Museum.

Where did it go, Rose?
I don't know;
away off, somewhere.

The fat hen
has left the nest.

I hand my daughter
this dusty book.
Framed in her window
the sky darkens to slate,
a lexicon of wandering stars.
Listen, child—the barking
in the distance
is Rab the dog star
trotting home
for dinner.

Applying to Bellagio

They take husbands,
but they don't take dogs.
Ridiculous!
and all because

they fear that barking
may disturb the muse.
Just ask Calliope.
I'm sure she'd choose

a silky spaniel
with a fluent tail
for inspiration, not
some human male.

I guess I'll have to stay
at home to write,
with dog and husband both
here, in plain sight.

The Art of the Dog

In Mary Cassatt's *Little Blue Armchair*,
it's not the child I look at but the Norwich terrier,
twin to mine, curled up on another armchair.
And in Picasso's *Boy With Dog*, I want
to enter the famous Blue Period to pat it.

There are dogs in the cave paintings in France,
and the hounds in the Bayeux Tapestry
are stitched into the scene by hand, chasing
their embroidered prey right into art history.

It's said that dogs in paintings
domesticate the scene or symbolize love,
that even a still life of flowers and fruit
may have a poodle or dachshund
hidden under the table.

Is a painted dog different
from a dog in a poem—from a dog,
like mine for instance, who follows
me from stanza to stanza as if I'm going
to throw a pencil for him to retrieve
instead of the usual ball?

Velasquez's *Maids of Honor* . . .
Madame Renoir With a Dog . . . Van Eyck's
marriage scene, complete with terrier. . . .
At night the museums echo
with the unleashed sound of barking.

Dog in the Manger

As if you'd keep your bones from other dogs
when you were done with them. What nonsense!

In any case, why manger? That Christmas child slept
in the barn with sheep and cows, not dogs.

And doggerel? Your bark
is so expressive

I think you'd choose a sonnet
with beef in it, if you could write.

Dog fight I understand, dog tired too—
you frequent the couch even wide awake.

But raining cats and dogs?
And going to the dogs—where would that be?

Why do I care? Language is where I live.
Besides, I have a dog in this fight.

Pluto

There's the planet, of course
with its icy outcroppings, its moons,

and plutonium, which will light our way
to the future, if it doesn't destroy us.

And plutocrat means wealth,
from the Greek, or power.

But for me it's the dog
with the shiny nose and the stand-up ears

who clowned his way through
my sober childhood.

Argos

Shaggy and incontinent,
I have become the very legend
of fidelity. I am
more famous than the dog star
or those hounds of Charon's
who nip at a man's ankles
on his way to the underworld.
Even Penelope wanted
proof, and Eurykleia
had to see a scar.
But I knew what I knew—
what else are noses for?
Men are such needy creatures
Zeus himself comes to them
as an animal. I'll take
my place gladly
among the bones and fleas
of this fragrant dung heap
and doze my doggy way
through history.

The Animals

When I see a suckling pig turn
on the spit, its mouth around
an apple, or feel the soft
muzzle of a horse
eating a windfall from my hand,
I think about the animals
when Eden closed down,
who stole no fruit themselves.

After feeding so long
from Adam's outstretched hand
and sleeping under the mild stars,
flank to flank,
what did they do on freezing nights?
Still ignorant of nests and lairs
did they try to warm themselves
at the fiery leaves of the first autumn?

And how did they learn to sharpen
fangs and claws? Who taught them
the first lesson: that flesh

had been transformed to meat?
Tiger and Bear, Elk and Dove.
God saved them places on the Ark,
and Christ would honor them with
parables, calling himself the Lamb of God.

We train our dogs in strict obedience
at which we failed ourselves.
But sometimes the sound of barking
fills the night like distant artillery,
a sound as chilling as the bellow
of steers led up the ramps
of cattle cars whose gates swing
shut on them, as Eden's did.

4 A.M.

I was the child until
my mother died;
now I'm the child again

afraid in the night
and sleep as elusive
as the past I cling to.

Old age is all
about saving what's left—
my father's heavy watch,

each tick a heartbeat,
my mother's initialed handkerchiefs
still scenting the drawer.

Buttons without
their buttonholes.
Combs with missing teeth.

I try to keep awake
all day, to sleep at night,
with only the dog

for company—his weight
at my feet holding me
to the earth.

But the sheets are tangled ghosts
waiting to dress me
in their ironed robes.

Marking Time

The dog waits at the door
for someone who is not going to come.
And the door waits
on its rusted hinges, not knowing
whether to open or shut.

Even the path, overgrown
with weeds and brambles, waits
in its own winding purgatory.

See me spending the small change
of my days looking out one window,
then another, for someone
to come and wake me
from this stalled dream of a life,
the way the princess,

in her flowery glass coffin,
was wakened by a kiss. Or the dog,
withholding its serious bark,
could be rescued
by the person it is waiting for,
if only he were coming.

I Sing or Weep

I sing
or weep,
it is the same thing
to the animals,
it is almost
the same thing.
The dog puts his heavy head
in my lap
pretending to know.
His small thunder
brings no rain,
no relief to the leaves
that wait poised
on their stems
for the first sign of wind.
What will their trembling mean?
I feel a mortal weight
that stirs
like some sleeping creature
in my chest.
Song wakens it,

tears waken it.
The nerves follow
their separate paths
to the same shady place
where once simple Adam
named silence,
named speech,
and the animals smiled,
the animals wept,
under their branching horns.

Renunciation

Like flowers
with knife-sharp
petals—

scions
of the sunflower
family—

the bright arrows
of beauty are aimed
at the heart.

So pain hides
in the billowy garments
of pleasure,

wounding
the open eye,
the listening ear.

An end, please, to all
sensation. Close
the museums,

lock the keys of the pianos
in their long, dark
coffins.

I choose an unlit room
and medicinal
sleep. I summon

for company, only my old dog
and, dim and silent as fog,
my old ghosts.

Life and Death on Masterpiece

I want to die an old woman
sun-struck in a garden chair,
my dog at my feet, the way Old Jolyon
in *The Forsyte Saga* did,
the bees around him buzzing

with the sound saws make
in comic strips to mimic sleep.
And just last night, Mountstuart
in *Any Human Heart*
reduced his past

to cinders in a bonfire,
then settled in his chair,
half smiling
with accomplishment,
and was gone.

They both slipped
into death so gracefully,
their shrouds of brilliant sun
half blinding us, their viewers,
in prismatic light.

And the choirs of flowers
in their robes of color,
the gardens sliding into afternoon,
all testified that life itself
could be no better than this.

Old Joke

The children all are grown, the dog has died;
the old joke says that now life can begin,
the creaking door to freedom open wide.
But old age seems my fault, a kind of sin
precluding guilty pleasures—food and drink,
the luxuries of travel, even books.

Depression is the bed in which I sink,
my body primed for pain's insidious hooks:
the swollen fingers and the stiffened back;
the way regret can pierce you with its knife;
the migraines like some medieval rack;
the winnowing of loved ones from my life.

For months I carried that old dog around,
helping her eat and cleaning up her mess.
Though she was deaf, I talked to her—each sound
the rough equivalent of a caress.
If memories are like the poems I wrote
but didn't think quite good enough to save,

and if the final wisdoms I would quote
await that cold anthology: the grave,
then let the sun, at least, become a shawl
keeping me wrapped in warmth until the end;
my lawn a place where children's children sprawl
next to the shy ghost of my canine friend.

Turnabout

The old dog used to herd me through the street
As if the leash were for my benefit,
And when our walk was over he would sit
A friendly jailer, zealous, at my feet.
My children would pretend that they felt fine
When I was anxious at some hurt of theirs
As if they were the parents, for the tears
At their predicaments were often mine.

And now against the whiteness of the sheet
My mother, white faced, comforts with the story
of Brahms, the boy, who couldn't sleep for worry
Until a chord achieved its harmony,
So down the stairs he crept to play the C.
She means her death will make a circle complete.

All Night

The children have gone
through doors so small
we cannot follow
even if we stoop

and the dogs bark all night
hearing calls
in registers too high
for our frail senses.

We follow words instead
but they are only signposts
leading to other words
leaving us lost

in our own landscape.
We struggle merely to see
for the sun too has slipped away
hiding its tracks

in afterlight, to a place of unimagined
reds and golds
a place where children

lounge on grass
calling to dogs whose barking
they can still hear
all these years from home.

Ghosts

We abandon the dead. We abandon them.
—JOSEPH FASANO

We abandon the dead as they
abandoned us. But sometimes
my mother's ghost sits at the foot of the bed

trying to comfort me for all
the other losses: my father longing
to be forgiven, to forgive;

the long line of cousins and aunts
patiently waiting their turns
to be remembered; the dogs

who were my shadows once
whining now at the gates of the afterlife.
My mother smoothes my pillow

as though it were a field of snow
ready to be plowed by dreams where
for brief moments my dead come back:

Jon as a toddler in my uncle's army cap,
Franny with the rosary of days
slipping through her fingers.

At times I wander through
the library of graves, reading
the headstones, remembering a place

where the ashes I scattered once
blew back on the wind, staining
my forehead with their dark alphabet.

In the house where I grew up,
the same sentinel trees
shade the porch

as they shaded the green years
of my childhood when my dead
were alive and full of promise.

The Ordinary

It may happen on a day
of ordinary weather—
the usual assembled flowers,
or fallen leaves disheveling the grass.
You may be feeding the dog,
or sipping a cup of tea,
and then: the telegram;
or the phone call;
or the sharp pain traveling
the length of your left arm, or his.
And as your life is switched
to a different track (the landscape
through grimy windows
almost the same though
entirely different) you wonder
why the wind doesn't
rage and blow as it does
so convincingly
in *Lear*, for instance.
It is pathetic fallacy
you long for—the roses

nothing but their thorns,
the downed leaves
subjects for a body count.
And as you lie in bed
like an effigy of yourself,
it is the ordinary
that comes to save you—
the china teacup waiting
to be washed, the old dog
whining to go out.

This Dog

Maybe I've chosen life—not just
the life of this dog I've rescued
from the shelter, but

my own life, mired in the same
books—Anna, Elizabeth,
Jane, the same

solitary walks—no tugging—
the doctors' offices changed now
to cacophony at the vet's.

I've chosen disruption and broken
sleep and the poetry of barking—
what does each growl mean?

how to parse the hidden syllables
of dogs, this dog? Maybe
it wasn't a choice at all.

Firing the Muse

I am giving up the muse Calliope.
I have told her to pack up her pens and her inks
and to take her lyrical smile,
her coaxing ways, back to Mt. Helicon,
or at least to New York.
I will even write her a reference if she likes
to someone whose head is still fizzy
with iambs and trochees,
someone still hungry for the scent of laurel,
the taste of fame, for the pure astonishment of seeing
her own words blaze up on the page.
Let me lie in this hammock in the fading sun
without guilt or longing, just a glass
of cold white wine in one hand,
not even a book in the other. A dog
will lie at my feet who can't read anyway,
loving me just for myself, and for
the biscuit I keep concealed in my pocket.

Envoi

We're signing up for heartbreak,
We know one day we'll rue it.
But oh the way our life lights up
The years a dog runs through it.

ACKNOWLEDGMENTS

"I Am Learning to Abandon the World" appeared in *PM/AM* (W. W. Norton, 1982); "Argos" appeared in *The Imperfect Paradise* (W. W. Norton, 1988); "Domestic Animals" appeared in *Heroes in Disguise* (W. W. Norton, 1991); "The Animals" and "McGuffey's First Eclectic Reader" first appeared in *Carnival Evening* (W. W. Norton, 1998); "In the Garden" appeared in *The Last Uncle* (W. W. Norton, 2002); "The Great Dog of Night," "Firing the Muse," "Rivermist," and "The Walled Garden" appeared in *Queen of a Rainy Country* (W. W. Norton, 2006); "Old Joke" and "The Ordinary" first appeared in *Traveling Light* (W. W. Norton, 2015).

I'd also like to thank

Catamaran, the *Courtland Review*, *Crysalis*, the *Gettysburg Review*, the *New Republic*, *Plume*, and *Valley Voices*.

"Departures," "Heartbeat," and "I Sing or Weep" appeared in *On the Way to the Zoo* (Dryad Press, 1975).

"All Night" appeared in *Even as We Sleep* (Croissant Press, 1980).